*L*ETTERS
ON A SUMMER NIGHT

Letters

on a Summer Night

by

Corliss Morris

PUBLISHING

Published March 2002 by:

KiwE Publishing, Ltd.
P. O. Box 28007
Spokane, WA 99228-8007
USA
Phone/Fax: (509) 464-1266
E-mail: kiwe@kiwepublishing.com
Web Site:http://www.kiwepublishing.com

Library of Congress Control Number: 2002101753

ISBN 1-931195-26-9

The collective works were previously published as:
Love And Other Images ©1975
With Love To The Monsters Under My Bed ©1976
Shadows ©1973

Printed in the United States of America

Love and Other Images
Original pen and ink drawings by
Ken Spiering

With Love to the Monsters Under My Bed
Original pen and ink drawings by
Ken Spiering

Shadows
Original paintings by Kay O'Rourke

Photographic and negative reproductions by
David Morris

Table of Contents

WITH LOVE TO THE MONSTERS UNDER MY BED

SHADOWS   Page

LOVE
AND
OTHER IMAGES

Original pen and ink drawings
by
Ken Spiering

Dedicated, with love,

to my Father and Mother

Artist's note

(page 27)

"To my lovely wife, Mary Jo, this portrait of you."

Ken

I want to be with you,

to talk with you about our days,

the journey along life's passages.

But most of all,

I'd like to touch with you,

the seasons of the soul,

love and other images.

Corliss Morris

Kindred Spirits

Come bend with me

And lean on thoughts

that have no words –

We need none, you know.

Kindred spirits

amid a world

of noisy syllables.

There Is A Road Deep In The Wood

There is a road
Deep in the wood
Where pine needles sleep
In the ruts so deep
And send their dusty
Smell to me, on sunshine
Perfumed air, so sweet,
I follow it's trail
Through silent trees
Which harbor chattering
Squirrels and bees.
Wondering at their chattered
Din, seeking to banter
And talk with them.
With eyes in the branches
My feet on the ground,
I wander light-hearted
Up and down, the hills
Small valleys and bends
Here and there, as thoughts
Touch tree tops, and
Balance in air.
The wind races quickly
To catch up with me,
It thinks I am lonesome,
But can't it see,
That here I need only this road and me,
That here I need only this road and me.

At The Airport

So close, so dear,

So far is near –

   A touch to chase the miles.

Be good, take care,

Don't go, stay here –

   A kiss to catch the smiles.

Come Into The Glow Of After-Love

Come into the glow of after-love,

> *Come close and feel the warm,*

That spills from my soul

> > *around and above,*

Come close, stay near, be warm.

Come into the glow of after-love,

> *Curl in, stay far from harm,*

That spills from the world

> > *if it knows not love,*

Come in, my love, stay warm.

Winter Parting

They stood, close-facing

Chins, in mufflers, burrowed deep

Snowy boots stamping softly,

Fashioned snow caves at their feet

Misty breath hung a veil of words,

Softly spoken, bittersweet

Winter's lace, a cool night blanket,

Covered gently, trees and street

Muffled sounds of steps in passing,

Fell on hearts, with aching beat

Frosty whispers, slipped through snowflakes

Mittened hands, pressed close to meet . . .

Through winter's chill

I hear it still,

As then it floated by . . .

So often heard,

An aching word,

One last forlorn, goodbye.

Corliss Morris

For Someone Special, You

To think you felt rain and laughter,

    the wind and the sea,

before I knew you

    and you knew me.

To think you felt joy and sorrow,

    love and regret,

the passion and tears

    you wish to forget.

To think you felt grief and triumph

    that you could not share,

before you knew me,

    and knew I could care.

Winter Wood

Is your life as winter wood,

   Cold, with circles tracing?

Etching fine, brown dusty trails

   Thinly cut and lacing

Symmetry of days on end

   Moments meant for facing . . .

Is your life as winter wood,

   Cold, with circles tracing?

Corliss Morris

If I Had The Time

If I had the time

> *to sit with you,*

We would talk of many things.

We would share old dreams

> *and wishes, then*

Enjoy the thoughts they'd bring.

I would search the new horizons

> *that your words would*

>> *bring to me,*

And I'd hope my words

> *in turn would then,*

>> *likewise, set you free.*

Lost One

Where is your home, little one

Why do you roam, little one

Where do you go, lost one,

    I wonder.

Who will miss you, lost one

Who will search, little one

Who will care, little one,

    I wonder.

Turn back, little one

Go home, little one

Stay there, lost one,

    They wonder.

Corliss Morris

The Taste Of Wild Honey

Memories chase the wind

    on a sea of green

Fields of sweet clover

    brush my mind

        as knee-deep I stand,

            remembering.

Pink lavender heads,

    heavy with nectar,

        bend with promise

Their sweetness bites

    my tongue.

Memories trace the wind

    on a sea of dreams,

        but the taste of wild honey

            has left my mouth.

Thoughts Against The Rain

Here I sit with my thoughts

against the rain,

Worn out, they rest on my lap,

like a broken fan

Spread for all to see . . .

My only company for now,

thoughts against

the rain.

1975   Spiering

The Barter

Night, my friend,

why can I not

settle into

your darkness,

and let

you

take me?

Alas,

the thoughts

of the day

barter with you

and win . . .

again.

Wind Watch

She stood just like a daisy there against

The garden gate, as tho' the wind had blown

Her back upon the sky to wait; alone

She gazed with eyes of palest blue beyond

The whispers of the trees, wherein she heard

With heart and soul, the answer to her pleas.

A prayer, that like her hair of gold was flung

Without a care, for its own sake, but sung

For one, by one alone, no longer there.

The wind whose name was wander-lust did weave

Upon the air, through trees, a song of hope,

Of love, for her alone to hear; I'm near

My love, keep watch my love, I'm near, I'm near.

The Vow

I entered love

with a sacred vow

You entered love

with thoughts of now

I left our love

completely born

You left our love

completely torn.

Corliss Morris

Come Gently Into This Our Night

Oh come my love, beloved one,

    come gently into this our night

Lean not upon the day, but follow me

    into abandon flight

That comes but once, if you are blessed,

    and with its passion brings,

All wisdom of life and its worth,

    more precious than the gold of kings.

However brief, our moment is,

    hold fast dear one, and look to see,

The treasures here, deep in my soul,

    as yet untouched and saved for thee.

With whispers sweet, I'll sing to you

    of riches, yet beyond your sight,

So come my love, beloved one,

    come gently into this our night.

The Question

When I find you

>*will I know?*

Will it be like

>*coming home?*

When I see you

>*will I feel?*

Sense a oneness

>*coming near?*

When I touch you

>*will you know?*

Will it be like

>*coming home?*

Will we know

>*together –*

>>*Will we?*

A Lover's Prayer

May love never be a stranger to you,

and night a welcome companion.

May you never be lonely in sunshine,

but know a lover's compassion.

A Beautiful Behavior

How subtly you rearrange my days

With soft whispers of passion that still burn

In a world grown cold, locked in steel-like stays

Of indifference; spirits still we yearn,

Living in our house of clay, to be all

There is to be, one to the other bound

As we are by flesh, our mortal wall,

We search each other's longings to be found.

With sweet surrender I rejoice to see

In your eyes all my questions put to rest;

Embracing your caress, I find the "we,"

An answer to all men's eternal quest.

In your arms I find God's gift to savor,

Love serene, a beautiful behavior.

Corliss Morris

In Meditation

I've lost my sense

of
    time
      and
        space

Here I am no stranger

in
    this

Another hour

of
    eternity.

With Love To Robert Frost,
Beloved Poet

You were here in the world
*   while I was growing up;*
If only I had known you then,
*   to take a cup*
With you, or perhaps I could
*   have taken your hand*
And walked a bit around
*   this earth you called your land.*
We could have talked then,
*   each to each, with poets' heart,*
For once our feet not shaky,
*   using words our only art;*
Understanding the pauses
*   we each took with care*
To side-step beat or rhyme
*   that forever lingers there.*
We could have walked among the trees,
*   your beloved wood,*
Exchanging phrases line on line,
*   and understood.*
A gentle poet, topped with
*   snowy hair, you were*
At home with rocks and fields,
*   and yet with words unsure –*
Not with their use or power,
*   but with the spelling –*
That bothersome form that
*   almost stops the telling*
Of some wondrous scene,
*   or great heroic fight,*
But for the want of one word,
*   lies just beyond our sight.*

With words we sit to paint,
    in vain sometimes it seems,
A mortal, mental picture
    of man's elusive dreams.
With life our only canvas,
    the ear a palette fair,
We stroke with words the senses,
    that thoughts wish not to bare.
We reach out from our pages
    to touch a listening heart,
If thoughts stir deep within one soul,
    we'll know we've made a start.
Along that road that others shun
    because it's not so worn,
We find ourselves, and others too,
    hosting souls unborn.
So we sit with pen and paper
    lone and set apart –
Knowing in our solitude
    the lonely quest of art.
You sat in rustic cabin
    sun-washed and heaven sent
To set your words on paper
    with which to make a dent;
With life's cold armor 'round us
    we vainly peered aside,
While stumbling in our darkness
    with slow, uneasy stride;
Your words, my friend, they found us
    and made us look inside,
Your words, my friend, they found us
    and made us look outside.

Hills Upon Mountains

Standing here upon this rise

I see hills upon mountains

And mountains upon mountains

Rolling on, oblivious

To the touch of my eyes,

and yet,

Beyond my vision, my soul

Is no stranger to the view.

Did I stand here before,

Eons ago, and look with

Different eyes upon this view?

Was my soul clothed in

Another flesh, foreign to

Me now, but at home then?

Or does my soul merely find

In me, a resting place

Before it travels on?

Is the scene before me now

Familiar to just one of us?

Possibly the hills know,

As they lean upon the mountains.

Those Who Covet

They scatter like leaves over dry, parched ground

They preen and they prattle with empty sound,

Brittle with wanting and not knowing what.

They live out their lives in an endless race

They end all their days with a line-filled face,

Brittle with wanting and not knowing what.

They leave what they wished, and worked for, behind

They go to their graves resentful, unkind,

Brittle with wanting and not knowing what,

Brittle with wanting and not knowing what.

To Look Upon Your Face

Your face, your face, the wonder that I find

There, is beyond all words I've ever known.

In your eyes I can see all my lost dreams

Safe in the harbor of your heart and mind.

Strong I stand to face the world, knowing that

If I should falter I need only turn,

To look upon your face, and from your glance

Will come a strength I never knew before

I found the haven of your love, your face.

Window Shopping

I have seen your face
    in store-shop windows
    reflecting on glass
    hazy with longing,
    not for earthly things,
    but for remembered
    dreams that are polished
    to a soft luster
    by years of careful
    wishing and dreaming.
Treasures of the heart
    sit silent behind
    your eyes and stare back
    with a knowing gaze
    upon their earthly
    counterparts, alone,
    reflecting upon
    reflections unknown,
    reflecting upon
    reflections unknown.

Endless Quest

Life needs

mystery.

To seek the

shadows

Behind the veil

of wondering,

is our ancient

right.

Knowledge stands ready

to explain,

but surprise

is evident,

when we find yet

another veil

beyond

> *the*

> *next.*

The Lovers

Wind . . .

    I touched them both and tossed her hair

        his face found silken shelter there . . .

        They did not feel me pass.

Rain . . .

    I spilled my tears upon his cheeks

        with lips she kissed them dry again . . .

        They did not feel me pass.

Sun . . .

    I spread my light around them both

        they matched my heat with equal warmth . . .

        They did not feel me pass.

Moon . . .

    I bathed them in my cool-white light

        and touched their world with silver dust . . .

        They did not see me pass.

Night . . .

    I took them in and hid them from

        all harm and thoughts remembered . . .

        They did not let me pass

        They did not let me pass.

I Ask You

If He can forgive you,

    Why can you not forgive yourself?

I ask you,

    Is He not the wiser one?

    The author of all thoughts?

    The keeper of all answers?

    The forgiver of all sins?

I ask you,

    If He can forgive you,

    Why can you not forgive yourself?

A Gift Of Buttercups

With spade in hand I searched the forest floor

A sign of Spring's first hope, to leave you at your door.

The earth is soft and moist beneath my feet

For rain of night has left its perfume sweet,

Upon the air it floats to me and brings

A message of its own and other Springs.

Soon there amid the moss and rocks I find

A cup of gold that winter left behind,

It holds some dew, a drop of liquid snow,

That melted when it touched the golden glow.

On bended knee I dig and with a prayer,

Thank God and Spring for treasures left to share.

For with my heart this cup of gold will be,

A gift of love, glad hope and joy, for Thee.

Contentment

At last I've found you,

I revel in your warmth

And find quiet in your

Velvet folds of peace.

If Only

I see the anger in your eyes

Questions, to which

I have no answers.

If only I could

Touch your cares,

Bind up the wounds

Left by a careless love.

If only I could

Stop time

Slow the days,

Turn back the sun,

If only I could,

Make you whole

Make you better

Make you one.

It Is Blessed

It is blessed to listen in silence

For in the quiet of a listening heart,

Can be heard the whispers of a soul lost.

It is blessed to give love in silence

For in the quiet gift of giving love,

You find yourself, your soul, made whole,

by love.

Your Glow

I see your glow across

the miles of faces

It reaches out to warm

and touch the spaces,

That are left by careless

words of harsh regrets,

Spoken by those whom love

flees from, and forgets.

Comment On A Comment

You say I am sad

that my face reflects

sorrows beyond you.

Your understanding

touches the surface

and goes no deeper.

If it could it would

see and find such joy

that the soul would be

blinded with the light

of a radiance

beyond you and me,

but not, beyond Him.

Corliss Morris

You Will Know Me By,

You will know me by

remembering how

I loved the wind, spring

flowers, and winter.

You will know me by

the letters I wrote

the sorrows I fought

the friendships I sought.

You will know me by

the songs that I loved

the books that I read

the words that I said.

You will just begin

to really know me

when I am gone, then,

then, you will know me.

Just Me, In My Nest Of Walls

There is no one here, but me

just me.

Beyond these walls is the world

and all

I know

But now there is no one here,

but me

just me.

As I sit here in my nest

of walls,

remote

and far

removed,

I know there is no one here,

but me

just me

And maybe just possibly

a bit

a hint

of you.

Triumph And Bouquets

I do not court adversity

nor do I run away

So when its done its worst to me,

I give it a bouquet.

No More Will You Drink From My Ruby Cup

No more will you drink from my ruby cup

   nor will I build castles in your mind —

     the sand is no longer moist, does not hold shape,

       like dust it falls through my fingers

     and rides the wind that once was fragrant.

Heavy with dreams, my cup was full to the brim

       with sweet answers — endless it flowed

     to you like the forever abundant sea,

        eternal with joy unending.

Now indifference rides the wind,

     with no fragrance in its wake,

       sand-dust follows,

         it is dry upon my tongue . . .

No more will you drink from my ruby cup

   nor will I build castles in your mind .

                . it is done.

A Love Song To Kauai

The breeze with windy fingers writes

A love song in my hair,

As thoughts and memories are tossed

Upon the fragrant air.

Vines green and lush with leaves that shine

Entwine to hold me fast;

A prisoner of lost dreams, I wish,

To stay without a past.

With ocean's roar a symphony,

The waves without a care,

Rise and break upon my soul,

and lay its passions bare.

Wind-Whipped Corners

The sound of wind-whipped corners

> *haunts the lonely night,*

>> *while dreams like lacy curtains*

>> *lift and sway against the flight,*

> *of wants that have no sound or form,*

but ride the windy night . . .

>> *in search of a listening heart to hear,*

>> *a gentle soul with sight.*

Hill Of Calm

I will stand upon that hill again

and view with steady gaze,

life's days and weeks

laid out below,

in fresh-green holly maze.

I will breathe the crystal air

therein,

and in its sweetness find,

all my worries and their counterparts,

wind-swept from my mind.

Ghost Fleet

Phantom ghost ships rode each wave

appearing in the night.

Their foamy glow a milky white,

against the sea-black light.

Their presence was a mystery,

and held by darkness there,

As fleet on fleet searched out the shore

then faded from my stare.

A muffled roar their captain was

determined of their source,

With unseen hand he sent them out

to search an unknown course.

The ghost ships joined in filmy band,

then crashed upon the shore,

As fleet on fleet appeared beyond,

to call — what goes before?

Time-Weary Am I

Time-weary am I,

>*Bone deep it goes*

Everyone knows, yet

>*Nobody knows*

How weary am I,

>*Bone deep it goes,*

Time-weary am I,

>*Soul deep it goes.*

Corliss Morris

Night Into Night

Come soft angel of the night,
>With your wings hold back the light,
a moment more,
>one moment more
Dawn is near the door,
>>Across the sill she stands and waits
>>>Envious of your silver night
>>With her spinning wheel in readiness,
>>>She weaves in golden glow . . .
But stay soft angel, stay,
>a moment more,
>>one moment more
For Dawn is at the door,
>Spinning, ever spinning,
>>Her golden net is done, cast . . .
But wait and hear me,
>Someday I will come with you
>>And leave day behind forever,
>And follow your flight into night,
>>night into night,
>>>night into night.

Two Old, Fire-Gutted Houses

Empty, vacant hulks
> *they stand,*
Gaping with unanswered
> *surprise.*
Carbon-black window
> *ghosts stare back,*
At progress passing by.
Twins of another age
> *set back, from an asphalt*
> *trail that leads . . .*
Everywhere, nowhere,
> *full of chuck holes,*
Hosting mud, night's rain
> *and weeds.*
Victims of civilization
> *they stand, mute,*
> *remote, but sane . . .*
For they are stationary still –
> *As we chase by to reign,*
For they are stationary still –
As we chase by in rain.

View From A Ski Lift On A Snowy Evening

The old men stood in

their age-white stillness,

parted only by

the icy night wind.

> *Robes of snow crystals*
>
> *was the garb of each*
>
> *member that made up*
>
> *their learned circles.*

>> *The moon a silent*
>>
>> *vigil kept to hear*
>>
>> *the wind-kissed whispers*
>>
>> *of the wise old men.*

> *With the mountain top*
>
> *their throne of wisdom,*
>
> *they nodded in mute*
>
> *reply to the stars.*

Silent men glide by

on icy cables . . .

questioning their calm,

and serenity.

Corliss Morris

Notes Of War

In fog-shrouded woods
> *armor shines*
> *horses prance*
> *nostrils flare*
>> *red with steamy breath –*
> *eyes wide with glassy stare,*
>> *see only mist.*
Anxious hooves tap out
> *impatient notes of war*
> *muffled sounds*
> *blend to touch*
>> *the forest floor.*
The wind whispers commands
> *to branches bare,*
Brittle answers call out
> *to the moist*
> *veiled silence.*
Women wait in stone-gray chill
> *cheeks wet*
> *with rivers*
> *of salt.*
Fires burn red and low,
Cold no longer knocks to enter –
> *For Reason is dead — to rule no more.*

Heaven Here, Mortal And Known

The smell of warm rain brings you to my mind

With a fragrance all of its own, and yet,

The oneness of your love and joy, I find,

Is beyond all senses and words I've set

Down on mere paper with pencil and pen

Full of the sorrow that I'd not relay

In equal measure your passion, and then,

Mortal as paper our love would not stay.

Bound as we are, by the limits of time,

Soon to be phantoms in each other's heart,

We rest on the touch of embrace, sublime,

Holding back with our kiss, the time to part.

'Til then my beloved, my love, my own,

May we find heaven here, mortal and known.

The Inheritance

You say you are no one, no one at all.

I would do battle with that attitude

And chase it from you with all the power

I have at my command. Then, with my thoughts

And tongue, would bind up all wounds, old defeats,

Made strong by doubting, and the foolish "self."

How we dawdle in our fears, laying claim

To each, like a lost heir, embracing his

Inheritance of dust and cold ashes.

How we kindle embers of past mistakes

With the breath of self pity and regrets.

If I leave with you one thought, may it be

That you are not of clay, or mortal dust,

But are endowed with an equal measure

Of spirit — unique, whole, immortal, now.

With Love to the
Monsters Under My Bed

Dedicated with all my love to my two sons,
David and Steven

to my nieces and nephews,
Corliss, Ty, Heidi, Katie and Roy

to my own . . . S. Monster . . .
and to the "child" in you.

Corliss Morris

Monsters Under The Bed

When I was a child, very small

I would curl up in bed

like a tiny ball,

So no one, no one, could see me at all.

I'd lie there so still, in a trembling

huddle, and reach for my bear,

to hold and cuddle,

As monsters filled my mind with a muddle.

They were there, those creepy, crawly things,

I know, I know, some were furry with

beady eyes and wings,

Just waiting for me, with their poison stings.

If I moved, just an inch, they'd get me,

I know, so I moved about, very slow,

and never looked over the edge below,

Because they were there, I know, I know.

First Childhood Home

To walk down that street again,

As seen through smoky glass . . .

> *a child remembering*

The door, its point peaked high,

Wood cool and smooth from touch . . .

> *a child remembering*

A fireplace, with mantle crowned,

Wood floors with sunbeams shined . . .

> *a child remembering*

Rooms dim with shades pulled low,

Closets deep, to burrow in . . .

> *a child remembering*

Narrow stars, with dark steps up,

Diamond door knobs, crystal deep . . .

> *a child remembering*

Plaster ceilings, traced with dreams,

Each crack a secret keeps, of . . .

> *a child remembering.*

Riding Home In The Car At Night

I love to ride home in the car at night
Curled up on the seat with my eyes shut tight.

To peek through the cracks of my sleepy eyes,
At the sparkling stars in the late night skies.

> *The tires crunch over frosty snow,*
> *Sometimes fast, and sometimes slow.*

> *Mom and Dad to whispers keep,*
> *Because they think I'm fast asleep.*

I'd love for this ride to never end,
But go on and on, and around the next bend.

Each curve in the road makes the car swing and sway,
Is home real close, or still far away?

Soon Mother will touch me and say, "wake up dear,"
That's when I know home is very near.

> *As I climb from the car and stand at the door,*

> *I close my eyes, just once more . . .*

And pretend I'm curled up on the seat real tight,
Riding home again, in the car at night.

Why Don't Fishes Eat Off Dishes?

Why don't fishes eat off dishes?

And why is the grass so green?

(Look at your knees, they're a sight,

And your hands are never clean.)

Why is the sky so full of blue?

And why are the clouds so white?

(Be sure to wipe your feet, my boy,

And please shut off that light.)

How do the birds stay up in the sky?

And why is dirt always brown?

(Oh can't you ever be still, my son,

And somehow settle down?)

Why are mothers always so pretty,

Mommy, just like you?

(I guess it is because, my son,

They have little boys like you!)

To A Sleeping Child

Small hands spread

    tiny starfish pink

On sheets, warm with sleep

I stoop to kiss them

    now moist with slumber,

    they rest, outspread,

    calm, serene, resting

    from a day of play.

Dream on, sweet angel, sleep —

    May I forever keep,

    The vision of you there

    Without a worldly care

Dream on, sweet angel, sleep.

May I Always See Christmas

May I always see Christmas

through my eyes as a child,

And stand by the tree

with wonder

May the lights always shine

through my senses as now

I view the gifts down and under

the soft sweet branches

Of forests green,

fragrant with joy and surprise . . .

May I always see Christmas,

dear blessed Christmas,

Through the child

that is in my eyes.

Corliss Morris

Sensible This, Sensible That

As a child, it was
>*sensible this, sensible that,*
>>*"put on your gloves,*
>>>*and wear your hat.*

Don't frown,
>*let's see a grin*
>>*pull up your hose,*
>>>*don't pucker your chin.*

Muffle a cough,
>*catch a sneeze,*
>>*say 'thank you,' 'you're welcome,'*
>>>*and don't forget, 'please.'*

Walk like a lady,
>*don't play in the street,*
>>*don't pick at your nose*
>>>*and keep your hair neat.*

Stay in your place,
>*take your turn —*
>>*Oh, when will you*
>>>*ever, ever learn."*

It went in one ear
>*and out the other,*
>>*those lectures and lessons,*
>>>*I heard from my Mother.*

But now I'm a Mother,
>*and it seems I can hear,*
>>*a bit in the distance,*
>>>*but none the less clear . . .*

Those very same words,
>*I heard before,*
>>*following my children*
>>>*out of the door.*

Small Treasures

Over the box of treasures he sits,
dear little head of blond hair bent low
With one tiny finger he silently sifts,
through treasures of long ago.

There is a large marble, but dented a bit
still shiny with bright colors lacing
Through bubbles in glass, suspended within
their hard, tiny round casing.

Through with the marble, his finger moves on
to encircle, then slip on a ring —
"What a wonderful stone, a ruby I bet —
must have belonged to a king!"

Bright eyes now explore each corner to find
that certain mysterious pin,
The one with the crest and the pearls all around,
with chains and a sword stuck in.

The pin was of gold, with letters of black,
what they spelled was a mystery to him
On the back was a date etched from long ago,
"With love to Mary from Jim."

73

With the pin in his hand, his eyes moved on
       to explore all the jewels, one by one
A pearl, milky white — there a diamond for sure,
       its sparkle winked like the sun.

The room where he sat was dim-lit, and still
       with shades low for his afternoon nap,
But he sat there absorbed, with his head bowed down
       the treasure box in his lap.

His mother peeked in, then with a soft smile,
       closed the door, again, to a small crack
On silent tiptoe, she walked on down the hall,
       with memories flooding back.

Wind

The wind, I think

    is heaven's messenger

The joy of it,

    that tugs my hair,

        warms me.

The Secret Room

Is this where they hid, when the Indians came?
Or was it a place for a "hide-and-seek" game?
That mysterious room at Grandmother's house
Where no one could enter, except for a mouse.
It just stood there so silent behind the wall
So that no one would guess it was there at all.
When Grandmother's dresser was in its right place,
With its tall, proud mirror that reflected her face,
All you could see of the door was one thin crack
That would slide open wide on a secret track.
One push of the button was all you need do
And then with a creak, it would open for you.
The air would swish out, like a dark chilly host
I was sure the dim room was "home" for a ghost.
I'd stand at the door, and stare in at the gloom
That clung to the walls of the musty old room.
The cobwebs were dusty that hung from the wall
The room was cut narrow, quite crooked, but tall.
I'd enter on tiptoe and peer all around
As my ears searched the silence, to hear the sound
Of footsteps and whispers of folks long ago
Who waited in dread for the raiders to go.
I'd stand, oh so still, as I'd wait for their dreams
But all I could hear was the creaking of beams.
Soon my head would be crowded with tales of yore,
And my thoughts would take wings like never before.
The room would be full of the battles I'd won
And I'd revel in praise of a job well done.
Soon day would retreat and the night would creep in
My daydreams would vanish, and ghosts would begin
To come back and haunt that dear secret, old room
That magical place of dark visions and gloom.
The door would glide shut with a swish and a click
The only sound now in the room was the tick
Of Grandmother's clock that stood down in the hall,
As it welcomed all guests, ghosts, people, and all.

Little Boys

Little boys like rocks and docks,

    Broken toys and noisy clocks

Strings and snails, and rusty nails

    Windy storms with lots of hail

Hats and guns, and secret rings,

    Little boys like just plain

        things!

Slush!

I love to stand in the sloppy, cold slush
While the insides of my shoes turn to mush
To just stand, and stomp and squish it around,
Is the best part of winter fun, I've found.

Now winter is full of all sorts of joys,
Like dodging snowballs that are thrown by boys,
But for me, I love best, that frozen slush
As it seeps inside my shoes with a gush.

To stand and look up at the dark, gray sky,
While counting the snowflakes as they drift by,
Is fun for awhile, but then you will find,
I have something much better, on my mind.

A marvelous puddle of deep, deep slush
Is waiting for me in the winter's hush –
So in I step, with a "smile" and a gush,
As the insides of my shoes, turn to mush!

The Dress In The Old Cedar Closet

It was long and swishy, purple, I think
Trimmed with ivory lace and ribbons of pink
It hung in a closet, on the top floor,
And smelled of the cedar, behind the door.

I'd creep up the stairs on silent tiptoe
Ever so quiet – so no one would know,
That for a short while I'd parade and preen,
No more a "tomboy," but a regal queen.

To open the door without a loud "click"
Was a job in itself – and no small trick
Once inside the small room, I loved so well,
I'd stand and sniff that sweet "cedary" smell.

There was only one light, its switch a string
To find that in the dark, was quite the thing
With the light safely on, I'd start my search –
Then sit on the trunk, my favorite perch.

The hats were up high on top of a shelf
They were lovely indeed, I'd tell myself,
With ribbons and plumes and bright shiny pins,
They had bobbed and fluttered in quaint old inns.

Then I'd spy that dress, hanging long and grand
and smooth out the folds with a grubby hand
For within the folds of that dear old gown,
I became the grandest lady in town.

I would walk and swish then head for the stair,
And slowly descend with elegant air
One step at a time was all I could take
I went slowly, you see, for safety's sake!

On the last step I would look all around
Then with dress lifted high I'd take a bound
And head for the yard in back with its trees,
Wherein I could dream and parade with ease.

Once there I would smooth each fold in its place
Then proceed to walk and glide with pure grace
Bushes and flowers would bow as I'd pass
Seeing just a "queen" instead of a lass.

I'd drift through the oaks, so stately and tall
Regal and grand, and not caring at all
Of the glances of grownups in the street
As they walked on by with duties to meet.

Not knowing that they, when they stared at me,
Saw dimly through tears, as they looked to see
Back in their childhood, a girl or a boy,
Pretending like me, and lost in their joy.

Maple Trees

In slim, gray sturdy branches
  a crown of gold would sit,
Decked out with reds and oranges,
  some browns and greens, too fit.

The leaves in dusty elegance
  would slowly lift and sway,
Blending with the wind of fall
  to make an autumn day.

I'd hide among the branches
  and breathe the frosty air,
Secure from eyes of those below
  who walked on sidewalk's snare.

There was a favorite branch of mine
  that reached out to the walk,
On tummy flat I'd stretch its length
  to hear the people talk.

They'd walk below with hurried steps
  completely unaware –
With thoughts their eyes were clouded
  from autumn and my stare.

How sad they could not join me
  and see my view, not theirs –
And dangle from smooth branches
  up high, away from cares.

I'm older now, but there is still
  a certain part of me
That searches out and climbs into
  that favorite maple tree.

When autumn calls I'll climb and sit
  in blazing quiet there –
Above the world with Fall, and leaves,
  all tangled in my hair.

Images Of: A Childhood Spring

Wet sweet earth

rich clumps of brown

topped with moss

warm green crown

    Tree-fresh wind

    damp smell of pine

    flower carpets

    wild and fine

        Biting breezes

        ear-pink cold

        sunshine days, blue

        bright with gold

New-mown lawns sweet,

my heart frees . . .

Spring is joy with

grass-stained knees.

Corliss Morris

Images Of: A Childhood Summer

Birds on the wind
> *hold sun in their wings*

White mist in the pines
> *on branches swings*

Alder leaves dance in
> *sweet summer breeze*

Sun shines silver on
> *pine-needled trees*

Butterflies glide on
> *air never seen*

Water and sun with
> *clouds in between*

Moon-silver paths
> *ride on lakes and streams*

Star-hung black nights
> *hold make-believe dreams*

Meadow-fresh mornings
> *crystal-blue skies*

Warm summer rains
> *catch deer by surprise*

A mountain of green
> *with my heart sings . . .*

Of summers of wind
> *and sun, on wings.*

Images Of: A Childhood Autumn

Sidewalk cracks
> *some higher than others,*
>> *crooked, tipped*
> *half buried in a blazing coat*
>> *of autumn leaves.*

Streets quiet
> *with lawns of green velvet*
>> *rolling up to silent*
>>> *brick houses*
>> *each different from the next.*
Sun shining dappled patterns
> *through trees,*
> *spilling patchwork quilt designs*
>> *on the ground*
> *in melted-butter glow.*

Faint ribbons
> *. blue smoke from burning leaves*
>>> *. lace through*
>> *tree limbs,*
> *tying with wispy stitches*
>> *the last rays of sunlight . . .*
>> *to the end of*
>>> *an autumn day.*

Corliss Morris

Images Of: A Childhood Winter

Icicles shining

crystal air crisp

plumes of air wispy

trailing from lips

Frost-crunchy whiteness

wind-kissed red cheeks

snow-downy softness

moon-silver streets

Snow-capped brick chimneys

angels in white

flying with arm-wings

in snow-sky flight

Stars are black nights' eyes

diamonds abound . . .

> *Winter's a snowflake*

> *on mittens, found.*

Alone In The House At Night

There were noises on the stairway
there were noises at the door
There were noises in the ceiling
there were noises in the floor
There were noises at the windows
that had not been there before
There were noises that made noises
which in turn made noises more.

There were noises in the basement
there were noises down the hall
There were shadows that made noises
as they laced across the wall
There were noises that would echo
as they answered each new call
There were noises of all shapes and sounds
some short and fat, some tall.

There were trees and bushes rattling
a thousand different cries
They were right outside my window
as they loomed against the skies
There were noises that would ride the wind
and bring before my eyes
All the shadow creatures of the night
with all their noisy lies.

I would lie in bed with eyes shut tight
        all covered to my chin
As I waited for new noises
        to come join the noisy din
High above me was the attic there
        dark-still and yet within
I knew there were noises lurking there
        just waiting to begin.

With my pillow up upon my head
        to cover up my ears
I would lie real still and think good thoughts
        to chase away my fears
Soon my Mom and Dad would come back home
        with smiles would wipe my tears
They'd pat my head, would say with pride,
        I was braver than my years.

I'm a grownup now, and older sure,
        much wiser than before
But when I'm alone, I still can hear
        some noises in the floor
Tho' they are few . . . what's that I hear
        behind the closet door . . ?
'Tis nothing there, I tell myself, still,
        I think I'll write no more.

The Carousel

Proud steeds on brass poles
  prance on air, their ground
With memories laughing
  around and round
Tails flying with music
  upon the wind
Jewels sparkling with colors
  hold rainbows within
Lights dancing in mirrors
  surrounded by gold
Shine back upon faces
  of young and old
Brass rings for hands reaching
  wait for each turn
As finger tips search
  for the gold to earn
One more free ride on
  the merry-go-round
That magical place
  where childhood is found.

Spierino

Spaces

Remember all those spaces
those strange and secret places
where our imaginations
could conjure up creations
which had the same weird features
of all those spooky creatures
that grew in those dark spaces
those special childhood places . . .
when our imaginations
weren't bothered with "creations"
and all the "second features"
were not just "boring creatures"
that filled up all those places
those long and lonely spaces
that our imaginations
could fill with <u>our</u> creations.
I miss the special features
of all those silly creatures
that grew in those dear "spaces"
those special childhood places.

Corliss Morris

Winter Dinners

Dinners by the fireplace

table on the floor

waffles crisp and butter-brown

Jack Frost at the door

chocolate hot, marshmallow-crowned

napkins clean and white

family laughter all around,

holds against the night.

A Horse Of My Fancy

Spring wind in my nostrils

       hair-mane on the wind

mind riding far reaches

       of skies-blue begins

to prance with impatience

       hooves pawing fresh ground

a horse of my fancy

       head high running proud.

Soft sunsets reflecting

       on coat shiny brown

star-forehead blaze reaching

       to fly with the clouds;

peaked-ears up and listening

       to catch on the wind,

Spring's song of sweet promise

       with manes on the wind.

A Sweet Tooth's Lament

You ask for chocolate

get instead –

A great big slice of

sugar bread!

Just My Kite And Me

All of me that laughs and sings
is there upon the wind
High above the earth, and free,
where secrets all begin.

I know my feet are planted here
firmly on the ground
But part of me is way up there
looking all around.

It may seem strange so much of me
is held by just a string
For after all a kite, you see,
is quite a fragile thing.

But it is strong, yes strong enough
to hold a lot, you see
'Cause most of me is up there too,
upon the wind and free.

95

Then

I want to walk down that road of "then"

> *to smell and taste life of*

way back "when"

the days were endless and full of blue

> *where every single hour*

> *or two*

> *passed with talk,*

and a friend that was true.

Drat!

Drat

    drat

        double drat

Mother Nature is a rat!

She gave me mumps

Lumpy mumps

Grumpy, dumpy, bumpy

Mumps!

Lumpy mumps

Grumpy mumps

Bumpy, grumpy, dumpy

Mumps!

Corliss Morris

Christmas Memories

Pants and dresses, stiff with starch,
> *still warm from the iron*
Ribbons, ribbed and shiny
> *cascading over square boxes*
Evergreen fragrance, laced with
> *Christmas-cookie smells*
Rainbow lights hung under eaves
> *heavy with snow*
Ovens warm and bursting with
> *turkeys, juicy-brown*
Aprons bright and ruffled, tied with
> *stiff, full bows*
Steaming mugs filled with white foam,
> *topped with sweet spices*
The tree, short and full, standing regal
> *rimmed with red lights*
Tinsel bells gracing doorways,
> *ropes of beads looped above*
The manger scene in gentle glory
> *near candles low . . .*
Fires send their smoky presence
> *up through chimneys bright*
Prayers and laughter, joyful singing
> *join to bless this night.*

A Child's Eyes

Do your eyes see as much as mine,

when my eyes look at you?

Eyes have a way of seeking and telling

all that is really true.

So say what you want and wish to say . . .

think each thought, through and through,

Yes, say what you want and wish to say . . .

My eyes will be listening to you.

Pretending

Look at me

look at me . . .

I'm king of the mountain

lord of the wind

master of mystery

and all that I see . . .

all that is possible,

all that can be,

is here at this moment

in me . . .

in me.

Corliss Morris

Halloween Night

Apples bobbing
> *black witch gowns*
sacks of goodies
> *trailing ground*
small feet running
> *scary cries*
nervous giggles
> *moon-lit skies*
smell of pumpkins
> *candle warm*
lighted doorways
> *ghostly forms*
doorbells ringing
> *down the hall*
arms outstretched with
> *sweets for all*
bowls of chocolates
> *popcorn too*
formed in balls with
> *candy glue*
high, sweet laughter
> *in masks hide*
eyes behind them
> *sparkling wide*
night of wonder
> *when saints meet*
magic words of . . .
> *trick-or-treat.*

I Wonder Why

I wonder why the sky is up,

and why the sea is down?

I wonder why a box is square,

and why a ball is round?

I wonder why the left is left,

and why the right is right?

I wonder, could the night be day,

and could the day be night?

I wonder what the world would be,

if what was wrong, was right?

I wonder why I'm wondering why,

I wonder why, I wonder?

Sam, A Dog

Eyes liquid brown

   with floppy ears

coat furry-warm

   to blot up tears.

Four dancing feet

   paws on my knee

his only wish . . .

   to just love me.

Thanksgiving Is:

Gentle hands and

smiling faces

all tucked into

fragrant spaces . . .

    Where God's grace is

    there our place is,

    all tucked into

    fragrant spaces.

Corliss Morris

The Music Box

*The wood is worn
          around the key,
a circle in wood
          of memory . . .
of quiet nights
          and wishing stars
of clean, soft sheets
          and doors ajar
of shadows high
          upon the wall
of whispered cries
          and mother's call.
With magic dreams
          of what could be
that tune now brings
          all back to me . . .
those moments spent
          with music sweet
when life was clear
          and thoughts complete.
With hands I touch
          its edges worn.
the circle there
          from fingers born . . .
within that box
          my tale is told,
the child in me
          will not grow old.*

A Country Walk

Sun-warm jeans

dusty, snagged

from barbed wire fences . . .

green branches,

leafy gates that snap

to hold me back,

back from the trails

that lead anywhere

away,

away

from the beaten track,

away from the place called "back."

The Old Farm House

It stood back from the road against the hill
That protected it from all wind and ill
Which could come from the sky, or hand of man
That dear old house, built in rambling plan.

An old gravel road led up to the gate
That opened on hinges with rusty grate
A path made uneven by rocks and grass
Welcomed all feet that were eager to pass.

Wooden steps that tilted and slanted down
Preceded the porch that faced toward the town
Wild roses would grow and twine all around
Lattice that went from the porch to the ground.

Beneath the front porch wild kittens would play
Hiding from eyes and the sun of the day
Then at night's fall they would silently creep
Out to battle the mice, to earn their keep.

In back of the house against the green hills
Small cabins would lean with moss on their sills
Near by was a bridge that spanned a swift stream
In ankle-deep crystal I'd wade and dream.

No secrets were held in the cool, clear creek
That flowed from the mountain's fresh forest peak
For pure was the water that flowed swiftly there
Over rocks worn smooth from the waters wear.

Wild geese and wild ducks in noisy parade,
Not caring what noise and prattle they made,
Would strut by the barn and call for their feed
"Now don't get too close," my Grandpa would heed.

In the old kitchen hung Indian corn
Just as it had when my father was born
Next to the wood stove it hung out to dry
Could be it was there to hear Dad's first cry.

The house has now changed since those early days
A new coat of paint hides old-fashioned ways
The steps are still tilted and slanted down
And lead to the porch that faces the town.

The stream is still swift and cold as can be
But its song on the rocks brought quickly to me
The wisdom of age, that all cannot be
As it was as a child, but in memory.

Be Not Earth-bound

Throw your hair and head

> *to the wind*

> *touch your toes to the sky*

Be not earth-bound as I, my son —

> *be not earth-bound as I.*

Green Apples

Green apples on the branches

Green apples on the ground

Green apples in my basket

Green apples all around.

Green apples in my pockets

Their juice upon my chin

Green apples in my insides . . .

They made an awful din!

Green apples, they were super

But not too safe a treat,

Green apples were much tamer,

Baked in a pie to eat.

When I Was Young

When I was young,

      I'd measure time

by the licks of an ice cream cone

When I was young,

      I'd spend my time

pretending and being alone

When I was young,

      I'd take the time

to enjoy all beautiful things

When I was young,

      I knew not that time

was truly, a most precious thing.

Corliss Morris

Letters On A Summer Night

Sitting by the fire bright

      with Mom and Dad close by

a lighted stick I find to write

      some letters on the sky.

With ember's light my only ink,

      the sky my paper black,

I draw some words upon the night

      and write my name in fire bright,

      then trace my name with fire light . . .

      to sign my letters on the night.

Rock Mansions

Many rooms has my mansion — how clever
                            the wind —
   a carpenter rare set his hand to begin
   with care how he fashions each room,
                    here and there . . .
   pansies, bright purple, climb rock-crevice
                          stair.
No walls has my mansion — how clever
                            the wind —
   he makes ceilings with clouds, then with
                    moss begins
   to cover the cracks, some worn deep
                      and bare,
   slender, green leaves reach from rooms
                  secret there.
No doors has my mansion — how clever
                            the wind —
   just air-walls are needed to spin
                  daydreams in
   a rock-couch is here, a lava bench there,
   with gravel for money, there's wealth
                    to share.
No bounds has my mansion — how clever
                            the wind —
   I need only this rock, time-fashioned
                    by wind
   with dreams and my mind to mold
                  memories in,
   with dreams and my mind to hold
                  memories in.

A Last Look Around,
And Then Good-Bye

The old house stood against
>>>>>>>>>>>>>>>>>>>>>>>>>> an evening sky
As I drove up the drive
>>>>>>>>>>>>>>>>>>>>>>>>>> for a last good-bye
I turned the knob and
>>>>>>>>>>>>>>>>>>>>>>>>>> opened the door
To enter a home that
>>>>>>>>>>>>>>>>>>>>>>>>>> was mine, no more
The rooms seemed strange
>>>>>>>>>>>>>>>>>>>>>>>>>> so silent and bare
Uncluttered, yet hosted a box
>>>>>>>>>>>>>>>>>>>>>>>>>> here and there
Old pictures leaned tired
>>>>>>>>>>>>>>>>>>>>>>>>>> against cold walls
They once had been grand as
>>>>>>>>>>>>>>>>>>>>>>>>>> they graced the halls
But along with the mirrors they
>>>>>>>>>>>>>>>>>>>>>>>>>> now silently sat
Staring at nothing but
>>>>>>>>>>>>>>>>>>>>>>>>>> skates and a bat
Each room, so familiar, was different
>>>>>>>>>>>>>>>>>>>>>>>>>> and now,
With the furniture gone, seemed
>>>>>>>>>>>>>>>>>>>>>>>>>> smaller somehow.

My feet wandered over soft
> *carpets now worn*
By hurrying feet as they greeted
> *each morn*
The stairs now so empty, no more
> *would they bring*
The sounds of feet running and
> *sweet laughter's ring*
The house now was silent, so
> *quiet and still*
Yet memories recall those
> *past days at will*
As I roamed through the rooms
> *in the soft evening haze*
My mind wandered back to those
> *dear old, lost days*
When time was forever, no clouds
> *and blue sky*
With never a thought to a
> *sad good-bye*
And childhood was dreaming,
> *as brief as my sigh . . .*
For this last look around,
> *and then . . . good-bye.*

SHADOWS

Original paintings by Kay O'Rourke
Photographic and negative reproductions by David Morris

For Kathleen, Margaret and Mary Jane

With special thanks to

Francine Donner

for her helpful information

and encouragement.

LOVE

Shadows

Why must my love

in shadows sleep

Through misty dreams

softly creep

Only to slip

quickly away

With the dawning

of each new day

Where we can find

my love and I

A place to stand

beneath the sky

Is there no such

place for us

Must all my dreams

turn out thus

Sadly I look

to my heart to see

The answer I knew

awaited me

My love who is beautiful

soft and sweet

Must always in

the shadows sleep

When I am with you

    there is no time

Eternity is no mystery

To love you is to be,

    all mortal thoughts, forgotten.

To Love Again

The laughter in you

Awakes my soul

From sleeping

It searches out

And touches

That part of me,

I thought could never

Feel again

Your morning softness

Melts the doubts

And fears of losing

The pain of hurt and

anger

Slips away

As together we turn,

(My soul and I),

in soft, sweet answering,
To love again.

Skin To Skin

The perfume of skin to skin touch

Blazes in delicate balance

As we weave our own melody

Of sweet whispers

On wings of passion.

Spinning, turning

Your flesh and mine

Joins the ancient wave

Of time forgotten . . . Love.

Enter Life Laughing

Enter life laughing
come hold my hand,
The wine is still young, my love

Enter hurt chancing
come taste my tears,
The wine is so warm, my love

Enter love touching
come take my heart,
The wine is so perfect, my love

Enter age sharing
come touch my soul,
The wine is now mellow, my love

Corliss Morris

To Grow On, Alone

You did not grow with me,
As I became a woman
The boy in you tarried behind,
Anxious to touch and taste
All things strange and different
The child in me,
(The girl I used to be),
Wished to do the same
But the woman called,
Her voice would not be stilled
I had to answer,
To grow on, alone,
You did not grow with me.

. Why?

I stand in a trance

On the brink of wonder

As I behold the love in your eyes,

Reflecting me.

Corliss Morris

My Love

My love is sunshine
> *warm green lawn*
>   *full of promise*
>   *like the dawn.*

My love is full
> *of joy unending*
>   *graceful as a*
>   *willow bending.*

My love is quiet
> *still and deep*
>   *a cool silver*
>   *forest creek.*

My love is pure
> *soft and sweet*
>   *moments spent in*
>   *velvet peace.*

My love is all

> *of this and more*
>   *my love my heart*
>   *an open door.*

Thoughts you send my way,

Open windows in my soul

Parts of you,

That are the whole,

Become a part of me

We are pieces

Of the other,

Entwined,

Making a patterned

Rainbow,

Against the grayness

That is life

Because of you,

I am.

Born Free

Proud beauty, fair of face,

Lanky limb, full of grace

Tawny mane, of the sun

With you I'd love to run

To touch the sky

To leap and fly

To be all,

Immortal

My words of how I feel for you

Pour out like anxious children

Spilling out of a darkened room,

Over sun-warmed lawns,

To race with the clouds.

Glad to be free at last,

From a soul dark with shyness,

They dart, then soar towards the sun

On wings of color and light.

Their passing is but a whisper felt,

Yet, they will live forever,

In the quiet places of the heart.

Corliss Morris

Spring, Love Renewed

Your joy-filled radiance

Has touched me

With soft, sun-lit fingers

My soul is washed clean

With your tears

Your warm breath,

Sweet with fragrance,

Caresses my cheek

My heart responds

To your touch

I stand transfixed in light,

All is radiance . . .

I no longer fear the night,

For I have loved.

MOODS

Corliss Morris

No Time

A chair, its lap full of sunshine, waits for me –
saying, rest awhile and you will see –
Those quiet moments I've saved for thee –
(But I have no time)

A rainbow weaves its colored hue –
through a rain-washed sky of blue –
Saying, look what beauty I bring to you –
(But I have no time)

Lashes fair, fall on dimpled cheek –
small hands reach, clap and seek –
Their love is for you to keep –
(But I have no time)

Where's the sun of yesterday?
It's with the rainbow, far away –
And the boy's a man — but they did not stay –
(They had no time)

Your Room, At Sunset

I went to the room again today

But you, of course, were far away

There wasn't a trace to show you were there

That you could laugh and cry, or care.

It's a simple room with a chair or two

And a mirror that reflected me and you

The bed's still there against the wall,

Was that your step I heard in the hall?

No, my dear, it's my mind you see,

It now and then, plays tricks on me

The silence is deafening to my ears

With clenched hands I hold back the tears.

My mind is flooded with thoughts of you

As I stand in the sunset's rosey hue

This room is empty, yes, that's true,

But my heart, you see, is filled with you.

Loneliness is the empty space you left,

when you went away.

Joy

It is boundless

Shining

Brilliant

Blinding

Shimmering

Glimmering

Never dimming

Forever racing

Reaching,

Radiance.

Fear

A cold, dew-laden mist

Creeping with the shadows

To obscure all things seen,

And reason.

Dipping, swaying, running, playing

Sunlit shadows touch my mind

Thoughts are racing, never staying,

To touch the corners, that they find.

Words

Words are puppets of the soul

With wooden steps,

They try to say all we feel

Painted faces – tho' bright –

Fall short of what we mean

For all their brilliance,

Something is lost in the dance.

Corridors

Thoughts,

Like ghosts,

Roam the dark corridors

Of my heart

The echos

Of their passing,

In the empty silence,

Bounce back

To fall against

My mind,

Weary with wondering

Of the unknown.

Dark Angel

Dark angel of the night,

    wings tipped with silver light,

What is it that you bring to me

    on silent tread, for my eyes to see?

Is it peace, eternal rest

    where my heart can find a nest?

Or is it blessed, gentle sleep

    that is your gift for me to keep?

As I slumber in your robes of night

    with my soul awaiting dawn's first light

I wonder which your gift will be,

    will I, tomorrow, still be me?

With Love To Life

I will bend, bow down,

> *rise again with the wind*

I will stop, go slow,

> *turn back and begin*

I will love, look up,

> *turn around with strife*

I will laugh, in joy,

> *with love to life.*

Our souls live in different worlds:

Separated by indifference,

And lost in the maze

of trivialities.

Prisms

I've watched the grayness come,

    slowly

Shadows no longer

    touch me

My mind floats in

    lazy haze

My thoughts are icy prisms

    dancing in

    the wind

They swing, whirl, touch

    and break

    into tiny

    crystal fragments . . .

        that are lost in the night.

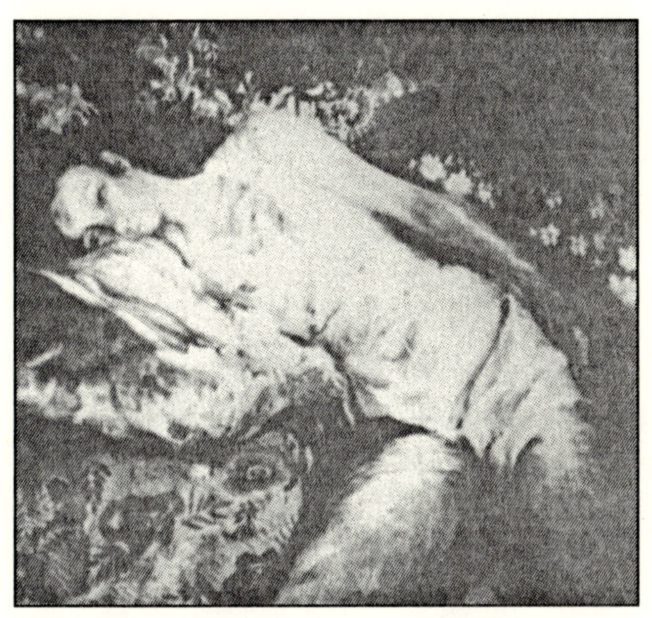

Gray Days Are For Thinking

We sit, my thoughts and I,
And peer at the grieving sky
I ponder thoughts that need the rain
To come alive and be again.
With my mind about me as a shroud
I never speak aloud,
As we sit, my thoughts and I,
To weep with the sky.

Night and loneliness are like brothers

   Each is cool, dark and silent

Tho' different in appearance,

   They are kin . . .when the heart is lonely.

Corliss Morris

A New Day

The sheets are still warm,

    fragrant from sleep,

As I lie silent

    on the edge of waking

My mind still floats

    a distance away,

      a misty object,

        yet vibrant

          with stirring senses

How wonderful to stretch

    yawn, reach out from the warmth,

To touch the coolness

    of a new day

The gift of night,

    given at dawn,

Is to be reborn,

    again.

IMPRESSIONS

Corliss Morris

Choices

Shapes on shapes

Voices to voices

Oh why does life,

Have so many choices?

Questions

Is it so strange

This questioning

We mortals

Ask one

Another

Why not

Turn

The questions

Inward

To seek out

A more

Important

Truth

About

Ourselves

Me

You ask me

Who I am

My mind hops

Mentally

From foot

To foot

I am,

I answer,

Me.

To love, is to care

To believe, is to hope

To have faith, is to know

To know,

To know.

Corliss Morris

To Music

Your silken web weaves softly

Through the enchanted forests

Of my mind

My soul rises with the mists

That hide the shadowed places

Your brilliance splashes

Against my very being

Spilling dancing lights

Over thoughts long forgotten

Together we soar

Above all earthly things

Alive and vibrant

For one magic moment

I am whole

God takes away things

that seem important,

so that we may see

what is important.

Man is a lonely

animal

searching for

that elusive

truth

that is

always

just beyond

his immediate

behavior.

The Search

Lonely faces seek noisy places

In which to spend their time.

With vacant eyes they stare

To find someone to care,

And share their place in time.

Corliss Morris

Visit With A Dear Friend

As we sit and talk,

Your thoughts tumble

From the soul that is

Mirrored in your eyes

They race ahead of,

And over-take, the words

We as mortals use

Soon we tire of

The complexities

Of conversation,

(The game of matching words to phrases)

And sit in blissful silence,

As our thoughts touch,

And dance rings around

Words,

That are better left . . . unsaid.

Child Dancing Alone

Lost in the sound of music

Your limbs were moved

By invisible strings.

I do not think you were lonely,

For music was your master.

Christmas is the joy

and radiance

Of all things wished for,

Realized.

Dreams

Night beckons

The thoughts

I ponder

With silent

Fingers . . .

    They slip

    Away

    With day's

    Last sunbeams

Mocking me

That I

Must sleep

While they play

Corliss Morris

Runaway

You stood
alone
against
the dying
day
Your shadow
fell
on wet
cement
>*beyond*
>*cold*
Your heart
beat
in sad
lament
>*take care*
>*runaway*
The shadows
of the
world
have sharp
teeth

Woman

No one will really know her,

or completely own her heart

For like the stars in the veil of night,

she's a puzzle from the start.

Corliss Morris

Olympic Tragedy

Tall young men with

  spirits high

Bodies braced to touch

  the sky

Wind and rain and

  laughter felt

'Til a touch of fate

  did melt

Their racing, winning

  reaching, driving

Full young hearts

  forever striving

Their glory brief

  and then a cry —

Our souls together

  wonder, why?

Reflections

Silken threads of sunlight

Grace thy face so fair

Deep pools of crystal blue

Hide thoughts I seek to share

Lovely lady of the lake

Are you really me?

Or are you just reflections

Of what I'd like to see?

You Said

You said you wanted this,

you said you wanted that

Your heart wanted everything,

but you gave nothing back.

You went on wanting all of this,

getting this and that

The world gave you everything,

but you got nothing back.

Deserted

It stands desolate
Against the sky,
Lonely
Boards, once brown with life,
Lean gray-white,
Worn from seasons' touch
Secrets on rusty hinges sway
With dawn the only audience,
As footstep-ghosts
Stir patterned leaves
Across uneven floors
They fall in dusty sunshine,
Swirl
And lift again,
With the wind
Finally, the dance of fall is over,
Ended
Hungry corners,
Dark with age,
Say, "welcome, enter,"
In cool, damp musk
Cupboards, stark and bare,
Lift dusty shelves
To hands and eyes
No longer there
Rooms, cut in dark imperfect squares
Echo whispers of longings past,
Prisoners in the chill
Yearning, the faceless windows
Stare in silence
At the setting sun

Corliss Morris

Day's last sunbeams,
Cooled by the wind,
Blaze for an instant
On cold glass
One last burning
Message of life
Reflects on indifferent fields,
Then dims . . .

It stands alone again,
With night, its only friend.

The veil of night

Slips slowly

Through the mist

Of a dying day . . .

Covering

All the dust

And worries . . .

With a

> *silken touch*

Of coolest silver.

Thoughts On An Evening Journey

I am — I exist

As I fly along the road

The late evening sun

Stamps, for an instant,

My fleeting shadow

On furrowed fields

> *(But the warm brown earth does*
>
> *not feel me pass)*

I wave my arms — move my hands,

As if to make sure that's me

To let the earth know

I'm here — now,

Alive

> *(But the warm brown earth does*
>
> *not feel me pass)*

But the sun and I know,

I am — I exist,

Now.

I did not find you,

My Lord

Until I had fallen,

Bloodied my knees

And stained my soul

Then I saw you

Standing there

Waiting

Patiently

At the end

Of the line,

With my

Former attitudes,

All forgiven.

Corliss Morris

The Soul Is Different

To touch the earth

and paint pictures

with my tongue

is a hopeless

task . . .

And yet –

the smell of joy

is new mown

hay . . .

the surge of love

is ocean's roar . . .

the countless stars

hope . . .

see –

The words are

familiar,

worn from use,

but the soul

is different.

Words are the rough tools poets use,

to etch a fine thought.

The words I seek

Slip through my thoughts

Like sunbeams

>*They are warm against*

>*My tongue,*

>>*Leaving traces of light.*

Printed in the United States
714600001B